HARRY JOSEPHINE GILES is a writer and performer from Orkney. She holds an MA in Theatre Directing from East 15 Acting School and a Ph.D. in Creative Writing from the University of Stirling. Her verse novel *Deep Wheel Orcadia* was published by Picador in October 2021 and received the 2022 Arthur C. Clarke Award for Science Fiction Book of the Year. Her poetry collections – *Tonguit* (Freight Books, 2015) and *The Games* (Out-Spoken Press, 2018) – were shortlisted for the Edwin Morgan Poetry Award (twice), the Forward Prize for Best First Collection, and the Saltire Poetry Book of the Year.

Harry Josephine Giles

Them!

PICADOR

First published in the UK 2024 by Picador
an imprint of Pan Macmillan
EU representative: Macmillan Publishers Ireland Limited,
1st Floor, The Liffey Trust Centre, 117–126 Sheriff Street Upper,
Dublin 1 D01 YC43
Associated companies throughout the world
www.panmacmillan.com

ISBN 978-1-0350-2521-3

1 3 5 7 9 8 6 4 2

A CIP catalogue record for this book is available from the British Library.

Printed and bound by CPI Group (UK) Ltd, Croydon, CR0 4YY

Visit **www.picador.com** to read more about all our books
and to buy them. You will also find features, author interviews and
news of any author events, and you can sign up for e-newsletters
so that you're always first to hear about our new releases.

Contents

for all my sisters

I raise my great foot over the city of speech.
My chest is bound beneath two straps.
The one is named diversity and the other is named inclusion.
When I sweep my arms through the thick air,
blessings fall to the folk below. And my foot
answers their prayer: silencing.

GENDER. This is a very small purple flower. It only grows in Orkney (the Orkney Islands, the Orkneys) and the very north of Scotland. It has two flowerings, the first in May, and another, the second, sometimes, in July.

SEX. Apollo flew to the bower where Dionysus slept and raised a bar of high-strength low-alloy steel measuring approximately 1500x200x75mm, and then she struck Dionysus several times until the god's head was a pomegranate and apple smoothie. A light spilled forth across the world, very bright and very loud; everything was good and pure and only the right things survived. I think about this sometimes in the moment before I send a poem to the printer, how before it is sucked through the rollers the squared stack of paper is as clean as a box of snow, and how on printing the lines are running off true? Aren't they? In any case, Dionysus surged back to life and there was revenge and suchlike, but the unreliable drivers for my Canon i-SENSYS LBP6030 often decline to perform, and whenever I get a new laptop I have to do a little ritual with a jar of bodily fluids and a dead bird before anything will print.

SEXUALITY. The bus advert for the news programme on the new Scottish channel, the one they're calling The Nine, like it's a team of Marvel villains, displays 'The New News' in blue letters on a pink background. Maybe salmon pink. It's just a shade greyer than Living Coral, Pantone Colour of the Year 2019, which embraces us with warmth and nourishment to provide comfort and buoyancy in our continually shifting environment. This itself is much redder than Rose Quartz, a persuasive yet gentle tone that conveys compassion and a sense of composure, joint Pantone Colour of the Year 2016 alongside Serenity, weightless and airy, like the expanse of the blue sky above us, bringing feelings of respite and relaxation even in turbulent times. Both of these colours are familiar to fans of the musical genre Vaporwave, an Internet-based microgenre built upon the experimental and ironic tendencies of such genres as Chillwave and Hypnagogic Pop, as a common feature of album covers, clothing and merchandise (although now that I'm checking Wikipedia, foundational Vaporwave album 'Floral Shoppe' (2011) by Macintosh Plus uses a tone closer to Living Coral than Rose Quartz). The point here is to explain that when Meryl Streep in 'The Devil Wears Prada' (2006) reveals that the shade of Andy's cerulean sweater (which is NOT cerulean, that's Pantone 15-4020 and is much lighter and softer than Andy's sweater) was selected years before as a fashion trend by experts based on significant collections by Oscar de la Renta and Yves Saint Laurent before ending up in a 'clearance bin', she overlooks the prior stage where Oscar de la Renta and Yves Saint Laurent were themselves inspired by Internet-based microgenres, or whatever the equivalent was at the time. In 2021 that *journalist* wore a Living Coral sweater more often than any other: may the coral consume him.

QUEER. If given Nectar, Thanatos will give you the Pierced Butterfly. And the memory of it is painful to me. The green fields. Reaching maximum affinity with Thanatos will unlock a scene in Zagreus's Room, where Zagreus can either begin a romantic relationship with him or continue as friends. And that fear motivates me to distance myself from the person in the video. The blue sky. Thanatos, Dusa, and Megaera can be romanced at the same time with no negative repercussions. I don't look and sound like that, do I? The white clouds. If Zagreus is able to fully romance both Thanatos and Megaera, another scene will be unlocked in Zagreus's Room, in which he, Thanatos and Megaera meet up and can begin a polyamorous relationship. I'm horrified and repulsed by the thought that I'm like her in some way. The calling, the calling.

TRANSGENDER. Have you ever remembered in the middle of writing a poem or doing the dishes that you're going to die? It's banal but also magnificent, this daily confrontation with death, scrub scrub, I'm going to die, scrub scrub, I'm going to die. Each bird flies through the day in the knowledge of death. Some of us die more readily than others. I have this plate that I recovered from a bin in St Andrews in 2007; it's very large and green, part of a set, and I've carried it to each house I've lived in since, perhaps ten. It survived the rage in which I threw every item of crockery in the house at the kitchen wall. One of my housemates is already dead. In the last year the plate has developed a very thin crack running down the centre (the bell sounds beneath the reservoir), almost but not quite entirely from one side to the other. It's the sort of crack that you only notice when you flex the plate in hot dishwater. I have to work hard to avoid flexing the plate, although flexing is the only way to check on the crack, because each flex makes the crack slightly larger (the bell sounds beneath the reservoir). It's such a lovely painful scraping bending breaking feeling. The sound of the widening crack travels up through my fingers into my brain stem. I know the plate is going to break one day soon and I don't know whether I can survive that.

TRANSSEXUAL. In the Rider-Waite-Smith tarot, the Eight of Swords depicts a blindfolded woman, loosely bound, surrounded by long swords planted in the ground, the ground which looks like water. There is a castle in the background. There are three swords on the left and five on the right. In the Tarot of the Silicon Dawn, the same card depicts a masked woman crashing through the wall into a nude woman's bedchamber and swinging a sword. The masked woman has a striped top, a skirt and tattoos. The nude woman is unconscious or dead, and there's a spilled cup of red liquid on the ground next to her. The sword is swinging in a blur; each instance has a different shape in a different elemental colour. It's not clear whether this is a murder or a rescue. In Thea's Tarot, a person is squashed into an egg-shaped hole in a rock wall bearing four swords on each shoulder. Their eyes are closed and their wrists and ankles are crossed.

TRANSVESTITE. I'm writing this poem instead of making my way through my assigned tasks for the day. I began writing it in my head this morning when I woke up, and then continued writing it as I cycled up Leith Walk (passing a bus with an advert for The New News) to go to a meeting. It was a fairly significant meeting taking place in the building which acts, in the 2017 BBC drama series 'Clique', written by Jess Brittain, as the foyer of the money-laundering abuse-grooming private financial company Solasta Finance, from which the heroine Holly McStay, played by Synnøve Karlsen, is ejected after exposing the scandal eating away at the heart of the city (Edinburgh), the University (Edinburgh) and feminism. Both the plot and the setting stretched credulity, and I found Holly McStay's expression of directionless distress, as played by Synnøve Karlsen, unconvincing as a means of conveying the horror of learning that all your ambitions and desires are founded on a system of rape. So at this meeting I demonstrated both artistic vision and organisational capacity, both radical ambitions and mature intentions, both drive and effectiveness, and I extracted from the meeting both information and action points which will assist me in my project of redistributing resources to make things that I think should happen happen in the way I think they should happen. Leaving the meeting and the building I was exhilarated, it was pouring with rain, I rolled down the hill ignoring the lights and letting the rain soak me, my life was progressing so well, and then this poem came back like a giant set of false teeth clamped to my neck, and when I sat down to continue my very ambitious and desiring work I wrote this poem instead.

TRANS. The lungs are not capable of inflating themselves, and will expand only when there is an increase in the volume of the thoracic cavity. In humans, as in the other mammals, this is achieved primarily through the contraction of the diaphragm, but also by the contraction of the intercostal muscles which pull the rib cage upwards and outwards. During forceful inhalation the accessory muscles of inhalation, which connect the ribs and sternum to the cervical vertebrae and base of the skull, in many cases through an intermediary attachment to the clavicles, exaggerate the pump handle and bucket handle movements, bringing about a greater change in the volume of the chest cavity. During exhalation (breathing out), at rest, all the muscles of inhalation relax, returning the chest and abdomen to a position called the 'resting position', which is determined by their anatomical elasticity. At this point the lungs contain the functional residual capacity of air, which, in the adult human, has a volume of about 2.5–3.0 litres.

Them!

They swallowed a small white pill and settled to write a poem.

The sun had risen an hour earlier, behind clouds.

A sentence is a subject, a verb and their ornaments.

They planned for the poem to narrate the emergence, in their
body of work, of poems identifiable as trans poems, that is,
poems which narrate the emergence, in their body, of sex.

To narrate sex is to perform disclosure: to open a door.

Many things may come through that door.

A book which has a sufficient quantity of trans poems is a trans
book, a book which gains access to and is excluded from certain
forms of literary attention.

A book which has content of strong significance to trans
communities is eligible for the trans literary prize, while a book
which is written by a woman is eligible for the women's literary
prize; both, however, must be written in English.

A legible poem is a poem which can be read.

To read, in literary studies, is to apply a given frame of analysis to
a text in order to produce new insight.

You read the poem.

You want to know to which sex the poet belongs.

You can find out if you like.

The sun rose higher.

They reflected on their sex.

On one side of their desk was a plastic organiser with six compartments containing their daily selection of make-up, while on the other side was an irregular heap of papers containing seven unanswered letters from their public healthcare provider: between these, they were writing a poem.

The shape of a poem is the shape of a door.

A door defines the threshold between one room and another.

A metaphor carries one idea into another, across the threshold between words.

A door can be open or closed.

A poem can be open or closed.

An open poem is legible, while a closed poem refuses reading.

A transition is a movement from one identifiable state to another identifiable state, as from one room to another, but 'trans' names both the state of having completed the movement and the state of being in movement, both the room and its door.

A transition makes public the sex that was private.

A poem makes public that something is wrong.

Between a waiting room and a doctor's office is a door: on one side, in public, each patient avoids the gaze of the other, while on the other, in private, each patient narrates what is wrong so that the wrong can be identified.

A body which meets a sufficient quantity of diagnostic criteria is a trans body, a body which gains access to and is excluded from certain forms of publicly-funded healthcare.

A woman who possesses the diagnosis of gender incongruence must be approved by a psychiatrist to be eligible for breast augmentation, while a woman who lacks such a diagnosis needs no psychiatric approval; both, however, must have sufficient funds.

A legible sex is a sex which can be read.

To read, in trans community, is to detail the ways in which the subject fails in their performance of sex.

You read the sex.

You want to know to which sex the poem belongs.

You can find out if you like.

The sun grew brighter.

They weighed their breasts.

On one side of their desk was a wooden bookcase containing five shelves of trans poetry books and one of tarot, while on the other side was a door: between these, they were writing a poem.

A poem is a collection of illegitimate sentences.

'Women's poetry' is a noun possessed by a noun, and 'trans poetry' is a noun modified by an adjective.

A noun is used to identify a class of things, while an adjective is used to describe a thing's qualities.

Carrying the idea of a noun into an adjective, or an adjective into a noun, is a common feature of English.

'Trans' is a political adjective derived from a medical noun.

The adjective 'trans' emerged through the interaction of medical case study, literary memoir and political action: three forms of narration.

To name 'trans' is to perform disclosure: to open a door.

Many things may come through that door.

On one side of their body of work were poems in which the poet was present, while on the other side were poems in which the poet refused to appear.

They can decide whether you appear in the poem.

You can decide whether to read the poem.

You cannot refuse to appear.

You are a public.

A public is a collection of legitimate people.

The sun was penetrating the clouds with some force.

In front of their desk was a mirror, recently polished.

From their position at their desk the mirror reflected a 1.5 inch-wide vertical strip of bright light reflected in turn from the windows across the street.

They refused to disclose to you the name of the pill in order to keep the poem closed, in order to refuse to identify their sex, stacked and split like an infinitive.

At their last blood test, their testosterone level was identified as 5.1 nanomoles per litre, and their estrogen level was identified as 293 picomoles per litre.

In the doctor's office, they were asked whether they wanted to change their medication, that is, whether they wanted to alter the probabilities of developing certain visually identifiable characteristics and of not developing certain other visually, that is, publicly identifiable characteristics, except that the research on those probabilities was minimal, and so they could only alter probabilities of probabilities, that is, best guesses, the lines between the medically measurable and the publicly observable stretched thin between data points, like a sentence between commas.

They refused to disclose to their doctor details of their self-administered medication in order to offer a legible narrative, in order to gain access to certain forms of publicly-funded healthcare.

As a result, they could not say what was wrong.

As a result, their doctor could not identify what was wrong.

They chose to disclose that something is wrong in the poem in order to make you an offering, in order that you might give in return.

A sentence opens with a capital letter and closes with a full stop.

The sun rose past the window, now giving only a diffuse and moderate light to the room.

You wish to know whether or not their breasts are metaphorical, that is, can you look at them.

You can find out if you like.

The sun's irradiance was identified as 25 microwatts per metre squared, and the cloud cover was identified as 7 oktas.

The desk measured 115 by 90 centimetres.

'Window', 'breasts' and 'literature' are not metaphors of identity, and 'sun', 'pill' and 'poem' are not metaphors of sex.

The poem was not completed, but narrated.

The New Woman
after Mónika Ferencz

derelict

~~raised~~   ~~forgotten~~ rockery

The new woman was born in a ~~neglected rock garden~~.

all anyone talks about   ~~truly~~

The new woman is ~~on everyone's lips~~   really

~~Everyone talks about the new woman,~~ but no one knows her personally.

like a red deer

boards   barefaced,   ~~deerlike~~   ~~wild boar~~

She ~~gets on~~ the tram ~~without make-up~~ and walks ~~like a deer~~

wild thing

winter ~~coat~~

the fluorescent city. ~~In winter~~ she grows a ~~fur coat,~~   pelt

and   hot

guard against   ~~from~~   heated stares

to ~~protect herself from~~ the cold ~~and~~ the ~~hot eyes.~~   concreted over

crammed

never cries   poured

The new woman does not cry. Her tear ducts are ~~filled with concrete.~~

menstrual blood   beef

No   no ~~monthly bleed~~   and a no-meat diet

She ~~does not wear a~~ bra, ~~menstruate or eat meat.~~

aborts

takes a wire coat hanger to her own

She ~~performs the abortion of~~ womanhood ~~on herself.~~

in

The new woman sits ~~on a branch of~~ a sycamore ~~tree,~~

changing

shifting pointillist

and watches the ~~pointillist changes in~~ the sky,

mull

chew it over

and does not b~~rood over it,~~

she   sweat   Moon

if ~~the moon~~ is too na~~rrow or too full.~~ ~~the moon~~   fat or too thin,

could

She ~~can~~ live her whole life without a partner.

lover   lover

she gets   she'd   partner   partner

If ~~it is~~ lonely, ~~it~~ prefers ~~to choose~~ a ~~mate of the~~ same sex,

she's planned.   a   marriage   y

but ~~he's been planning his~~ honeymoon with celestial bod~~ies~~ since childhood.

dazzling

glittering snow

The new woman bathes at night in the ~~brilliant snowfall~~

glorious

she   the   ~~carelessness~~

and falls asleep in a cathedral of ~~frivolity.~~

carefree   carefreeness

careless

gay

The New Woman

after Mónika Ferencz

The new woman was born in a derelict rockery.

The new woman is all anyone talks about, but no one knows her personally.

She boards the tram barefaced and like a red deer walks

the fluorescent city. She grows a winter pelt

to guard against the cold and the hot stares.

The new woman doesn't cry. Her tear ducts are concreted over.

No bra, no menstrual blood and a no-meat diet.

She aborts her own womanhood.

The new woman sits in a sycamore,

and watches the changing pointillist sky,

and doesn't sweat

if she's too fat or too thin, the Moon.

She could live her whole life without a partner.

If she gets lonely she'd prefer a same-sex lover,

but since childhood she's planned her honeymoon with a celestial body.

The new woman bathes at night in the glorious snow

and in the gas cathedral she falls asleep.

The New Girl

after Mónika Ferencz

The new girl was born in a derelict rockery.
Her mother was a spider and her other mother was a
   sharp-toothed bird.
Her infancy was cruel, her childhood was coddled,
and her adolescence required a sterner hold. The new girl is
   expanding.
The new girl is ineffective. She cannot be escaped.
The new girl is all anyone talks about, but no one knows her
   personally.
The new girl won't shut up, but no one understands her.
Her tongue is made from iron. She won't stop eating gold.
The new girl cannot sleep. The new girl cannot wait.
She boards the tram barefaced and like a red deer walks
the fluorescent city. She grows a winter pelt
to guard against the cold and the hot stares.
Her hooves are manufactured abroad. The new girl's horns
are mounted over her own mantlepiece.
The new girl doesn't cry. Her tear ducts are concreted over.
Her pores are scrubbed with goat's milk. Her nails are knives.
Her vagina never heals. Her navel is a portal to purgatory.
Her breasts are an auto-immune response.
Her filters are undeclared. Her tuck drops from a height.
Her nostrils are a woodland grove. Her brow
has lost its best bones. No sense of smell. No power of flight.
No bra, no menstrual blood and a no-meat diet.
No heels, no hips, no skill at mending. No sense of tenderness.
No justification for her absence. No status.
She aborts her own womanhood.
She takes a wire coat hanger to her own femininity.
She delivers her muliebrity to the family planning clinic.

She self-administers a mifepristone–misoprostol combination
   regimen
to treat her body dysmorphia disorder.
She travels a thousand miles to have her gender removed.
The new girl can order these medications on the internet.
She can receive these treatments without supervision.
She is on the dark web. Her legs pluck the strings.
The new girl is worsening.
The new girl sends death threats.
She curses, she won't have sex,
she is too old for childbirth.
She learned too much too young.
The new girl sleeps till noon.
The new girl stretches for the camera.
The new girl sits in a sycamore,
and watches the changing pointillist sky
and doesn't sweat
if she's too fat or too thin, the Moon.
She could live her whole life without a partner.
She could be happy without starting a family.
She could forget her parents and be none the poorer.
She could abandon her elders and thrive.
She might never die.
If she gets lonely she'd prefer a same-sex lover,
but since childhood she's planned her courtship with the
   ocean,
her marriage to the wind,
and her honeymoon with a celestial body.
The new girl bathes at night in the glorious snow,
and in the gay cathedral she falls asleep.

Materials

Each day the world was more girls. Each day greener
and deeper and: brickwork, girls; bin lorry, girls;
three loaves, three girls; vitamin supplements, girls
rattling bones in the morning coop. We were girls.

We grieved. We bit. We waded from girls to women
and were girls anew: sticky, sorrowful, spite
tucked intimate like cool calzone. We
ejected from girls to men and were girls anew,

violent smooth. Girls whooped out those 'Young-Girl's
way of being is to be nothing' guys,
those guys! Those guys ratioed by the specific
labour of their girlhoods, pores and butter.

At any rate: more girls, more peace. No?
Why else does girls the triple goddess grant
to the incandescent pavement, whyever else
the warheads girls, cyclopean, under desert?

Fingers are too much girls to tell any further.
Each good day the words more girls, and louder.

I Love to Hear Her Speak

a cling peach slithering out from its tin

a lip gloss ground into paste by the teeth

a burnt clutch scribbling down from the pass

a cowpat drilled by extravagant heels

a hangnail snatching a lark by the throat

a wire thong under a cage crinoline

a crazed screen slicing a covetous thumb

a quotetweet high on the sodium moon

a plum duff smelting its thruppenny bit

a lightbulb loose in a bucket of knives

a string cheese stubbornly whole in the pipes

a war pig through the dimensional gate

a salt lick slapping a jellyfish sting

a blessed bass warily bowed at the bridge

Why do we not everywhere see innumerable transitional forms? Why is not all nature in confusion?

But Charlie, I vary a body:
deforest my face and force
volcanos from my chest.
May I stroke your liberal beard
in survival? May you and the lads
see me pass saying fit, fit, fittest?

Ach, Charlie! My gametes
rest in their holsters, never
to be unslung, be sprung,
be origin, be stringing
descent. (Selection is choice
and coercion.) The proof of me

is a finch, two finches, eighteen
finches (vegetarian,
vampire, large ground, small ground,
grey) known for their marked
profusion of beak form and function.
A charm, a trembling, a trimming.

Oh Charlie, the flock of me settles
the branches of your damned
ineluctable equation,
twittering . . . Please, Charlie!
Forgive the annotation.
Favour the preservation.

May a Transsexual Hear a Bird?

May a transsexual hear a bird?
When I, a transsexual, hear a bird,
I am a transsexual hearing a bird;
when you hear a bird you are
a person hearing a bird. That is,
I am specific, you are general.
When a bird sounds in a poem
it is a symbol of hearing a bird,
a symbol of a person being
in relation to nature. Only
a person may hear this. Only a person
may hear a bird and write a poem
on hearing a bird and in so doing
praise the gentle dissolution
of personhood or elsewise strive
towards the clear and questionless presence
of an unworded bird, being.
Were I to attempt such a poem again,
I would be a transsexual writing
a poem on hearing a bird – I note
that 'transsexual' is the legal
adjective for a person with
the protected characteristic of
'gender reassignment' in
the Equality Act (2010),
Section 7, which applies
to any person at any stage

of changing any aspect of sex,
and so to make a claim of employment
discrimination I must have
the capital, social and economic,
to bring such a claim and also be
a transsexual – hence incapable
of dissolving without addressing
my transsexuality to the bird.
Even were I to fail to sound
out my transsexuality,
it would remain in the title, unsilent,
a framing device, regardless, and so
once again you would be hearing
a transsexual hearing a bird.
But now I am too preoccupied
with how to source testosterone –
a Class C Controlled Substance
under the Misuse of Drugs Act
(1971) carrying,
for supply, a maximum tariff
of fourteen years' imprisonment,
and/or a heavy fine – to give
to my friend, and how to publish a zine
detailing how to negotiate
and circumvent the Gender Identity
Clinic system, given waiting
times for first appointments now
range from three to seven years,
without attracting the critical social
media attention that would shut down

any explicit alternative routes,
and whether the fact I have not heard
from my trans sister in over a month
means she is in a severe mental
health crisis or merely working,
and whether I have the strength and love
to call her, to remember to hear
a bird. If I cannot remember
to hear a bird I cannot write
a poem. How can I lack the strength
and love to call? Because I have not
heard enough birds. Because I am scared
of what it will mean if she answers. Because
I am scared of what it will mean if she doesn't.
Because I have been working in far
too many political meetings scolding
parliamentarians to call
or hear a bird. I tilt the window
on its catch so I, a transsexual,
may hear the birds singing. If I
may hear the birds singing the sound
may lift me from myself and my
working conditions. Then the self,
the conditions, and the listening day.

The Worker

SOLAN STABBAN INTAE FYSHLESS JABBUL # SILLER SMOWT BIRLAN I'THE BEN-BANKIT KAEJ

The worker is taking a mid-morning shower and assessing her life, her work, and whether it can continue.

The worker cannot explain her job to a taxi driver, but she is so busy, so busy: this is what she says when asked how she is, 'So busy.'

The worker's busy working life consists mostly of emails: she emails to pitch for work; she responds to emails soliciting her work; to do her work, she emails people to ask them to do work; sometimes she sends longer emails containing advice, ideas and spreadsheet attachments.

The worker, in between emails, checks Twitter, the hashtag #fullcommunism, which is what she tweets when she is unhappy, which is always: 'Ran out of hot water halfway through my shower #fullcommunism'; '#fullcommunism with a three hour delay on the morning chorus as a transitional demand'.

The worker is aware that the disjuncts between her ironic deployment of radical political terminology, the record of totalitarian state violence under the same terminology and the clear need for revolutionary political change are, at the very least, problematic, but these disjuncts ease her horror, which is acute.

The worker does not know how to properly and responsibly account for the relationship between, on the one hand, the immediacy of her acute personal horror, and, on the other,

BAALPYNT SKYTAN AFF THE KONFRENS TAEBUL # GEUD WIRDS RASHAN OOT O ORAFU MULLS

horror on a global political scale; she is in fact gnawed by the question of whether her acute and terrible horror – which manifests as purely psychological, insofar as the material and the psychological can be disentangled, insofar as they are not, in the immediacy of her own acute, terrible and unbearable horror, entirely co-constituted – whether her acute, terrible, unbearable but deeply solipsistic horror can be compared to or accounted for by the same socioeconomic formulations as disease, famine, war and death.

The worker is rinsing conditioner from her hair, and then realises she has already done so, and so is rinsing already-rinsed hair.

The worker does not have a job.

The worker gets paid irregularly for a range of tasks encompassing management, consultation and creative development; she has two degrees and last year her total income after business expenses was less than the minimum wage.

The worker frequently spends the morning sobbing.

The worker frequently spends the afternoon in bed numbed by those American drama serials, pirated on her high-speed Wi-Fi, that offer that precisely-engineered balance between clever and stupid which enables immersive escapism without an excess of blank rage.

The worker is not clear as to how she is able to afford high-speed Wi-Fi and a thick duvet on her objectively insufficient income, and yet she can; perhaps it is because she does not have children; perhaps it is because she barely eats.

The worker draws on scraps of paper careful sketches of urban wildlife, and these creative interludes are what the worker uses to justify her life: there are moments of drawing in which 'peace' is something more than an abstract noun.

The worker's parents own their own house outright.

The worker does not live there.

The worker values her independence.

The worker has had her eyes closed for the last five minutes, enjoying the sense of nullity that comes from falling water; she keeps her eyes closed.

The worker took an old friend to the pub last night – an old friend whom the worker has always wanted to sleep with, both in the sense of having sex with and in the sense of entering several hours of warm oblivion with, but who through a thousand signals has made it clear they do not find the worker sexually attractive, at least according to the worker's understanding, which cannot encompass the thought that anyone would find her attractive, raising the question of whether the signals are transmitted or merely received, a question that is nonetheless moot given the impossibility of acting on any of its possible answers – and explained at length to that friend in the pub how all of her work, the emails, the emails about emails, was an elaborate mechanism for providing economic support to those experiments in drawing which provide her only respite from 'the screaming'.

The worker said, "I want to be an artist," and her friend said, "You are one already," and the worker said, "No."

The worker believes firmly in the necessity of a strong welfare state, and perhaps even in the strategic facility of a Universal Basic Income in order to provide a base level of comfort and security to every human individual so that they are able to pursue their self-fulfilment, except insofar as it applies to herself; that is to say, the worker will happily attend a protest march in defence of doctors' salaries (this is not true, she will not be happy on attending, she will be anxious and afraid, but will still attend), and is fervent about fighting for the happiness of every human individual on the planet except for herself.

The worker is fully aware of this contradiction, and nonetheless explained to her friend that the only thing that would make her feel more vain, more self-indulgent, more useless to society than her current work would be calling herself an 'artist'.

The worker's friend held the worker's arm.

The worker experiences instances when she can locate her potential for happiness within a coherent political discourse: the moment when her friend held the worker's arm was one such.

The worker's friend, with extraordinary gentleness, let go.

The worker opens her eyes and turns off the shower and stands very still, with her body held open, dripping.

The worker's contracts are not regular.

The worker does not have a pension or sick leave.

The worker begins to shiver as the water evaporates from her skin.

The worker has friends who refer to this form of work as 'precarious', but she is suspicious of this terminology, uncertain as to whether it is truly a different labour system to that of the nineteenth-century industrial working class on whom Marxist economics was predicated.

The worker's shivering causes her to bend at the knees.

The worker returns often to a mental image of anonymous hordes of men in flat caps queueing outside factory gates, waiting for work, in order to compare that image to an image of her inbox.

The worker understands that she should step out of the shower, and although the distance between 'shivering' and 'stepping out of the shower' is impossible there is somewhere a voice reminding the worker to count her breaths.

The worker wonders whether 'precarity' is the name that people with middle-class backgrounds and training give to their situation in order to emotionally distance themselves from those swarming men and their forms of struggle, and so whether the defining characteristic of contemporary precarity is simply that its workers have been promised an exit which has never appeared, and indeed several of the worker's friends refer to themselves as 'precarious workers' when the worker is well aware that they have savings accounts, wealthy parents and/or University-level education, granting them resources, skills and social markers essential to negotiating the world's financial tortures far beyond those usually attributed to what the worker thinks of as the 'real' working class, whom the worker rarely meets.

The worker said as much last night in the pub to her friend, who fell silent.

The worker remembered then, with a burst of psychic pain, that her friend had wealthy parents with whom they did not speak, could not speak since those parents' refusal to accept their 'lifestyle'.

The worker, at that moment, turned back to her friend with her lips shaking, and the prehistoric terror in the worker's eyes was so deep and all-absorbing that her friend bit down their anger, shook their head and said, "It's OK, really, it's OK."

The worker counts; the worker counts; the worker counts.

The worker felt that it was not OK, would never be OK.

The worker at that point in the conversation launched into a familiar cycle of self-loathing, aware that her level of self-loathing and her ability to project that self-loathing onto others was itself loathsome, but also unable to turn that awareness towards overcoming self-loathing, meaning that that awareness was itself a source of further loathing, and that any attempt to explain this to her friend would be further reason to be loathed.

The worker thus, after a frail extension of the conversation in which she attempted to comfort her friend for her friend's inability to provide true comfort without verbally acknowledging that either of them required or was asking for comfort from the other, hugged her friend and went home, turning the corner before she began to cry.

The worker, counting, steps out of the shower and reaches for her towel.

The worker believes that her brightest times have been those when she has been able to construe her horror (acute, terrible, unbearable, insurmountable) as a product of 'neoliberalism', when she has been able to blame neoliberalism for the destruction of geographically local community, perpetuation of permanent terror and anxiety, dependence on chronic debt, complicity in international warfare, constant forms of normative violence and overall atmosphere of dread which are the cause of the horror which is in this moment threatening her life.

In this moment, indeed, hanging her towel on the radiator and pulling on a t-shirt and shorts, one such instant of clarity provides the worker with enough impetus for her to sit at her desk, open her laptop and get to work.

Living

Ace of Wands

Spells are desires in clear enough action
to turn the elements. Here is a spell:
when the bargain we are made to make
for food and shelter is to force
our bodies beyond their own wants, to place
the gold of our agency at the service
of another's thirst, to give up the gifts
of time and breath to clocks and smoke,
then those who say they value life
shall pay in return enough for life.
And when you do not we will take it.

Ace of Cups

Ace of Swords

Ace of Pentacles

saltsaltsaltsaltsaltsaltsaltsaltsaltsaltsaltsaltsaltsaltsaltsaltsaltsaltsaltsaltsaltsaltsaltsaltsaltsaltsaltsaltsaltsaltsaltsaltsaltsaltsaltsaltsaltsaltsaltsaltsaltsaltsaltsaltsaltsaltsaltsaltsaltsaltsaltsaltsaltsaltsaltsaltsaltsaltsaltsaltsaltsaltsaltsalt

A scan of the ashes of the ritual in
which I began hormone therapy,
which I was suppe███to bury in a
safe and █████ ████ ██t which
I forgo█ ███████ ███████ ███dwich
bag in ████████ ███████ █████until
last ███ ████████ ███████ ████was
referre█ ████████ ███████ ███tity
Clinic█ ████████ ███████ ███ took
ove█ ████████ ███████ ████hoped
to s██p██ ███ ██████ ███ ██ic fell
around ████ ███ ███ ri█ ████ned,
when I ███████ ██ from the
crossing of███ █████rive and the
Water of Leith, █ █ning into the
sea, before a storm, watched by
young eiders.

A pair of bronze
clamps found in the
River Thames near
London Bridge in
1840, perhaps broken
and captured by
Christians raiding
the Temple of the
Magna Mater Cybele,
who adorns them
alongside her lover,
Attis, the very
other god, and which
were used the
ritual of
her priests, the galli,
in these islands, and
which I in
the hour before my
appointment with a
private surgeon, who
measured my skull,
who confirmed the
surgery the state
would not, whom
I paid so that I
could a prayer
to someone who
believed.

The story in my
school was that
the way to obtain
Mew, the original
and more powerful
Pokémon whom
Mewtwo had been
cloned, vicious in its
genderless lateness,
was to play the
game exactly one
hundred s and
then that moment
go to specific cave
where you could
have one chance
to red the psychic
kitten to
as close was
possible at which
point a ultra
the most powerful
pokéball would
succeed in ding
Mew to your service.
In my room it was
midnight when one
hundred hours
and Mew did no

Gender Reassignment Protocol   January 2012

Gender Reassignment Protocol

When walking the broad glen path, the stick will be a full participant in decisions about your pacing and direction and can speak any thought the hand needs in order to do so.

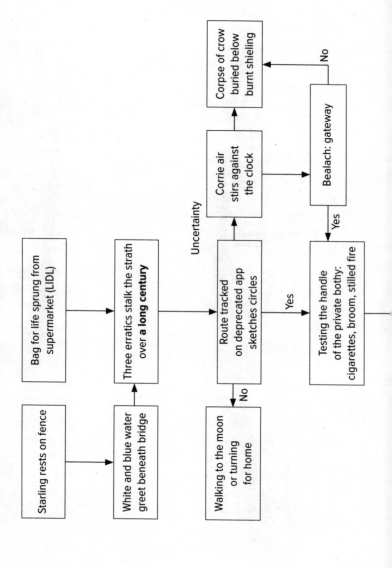

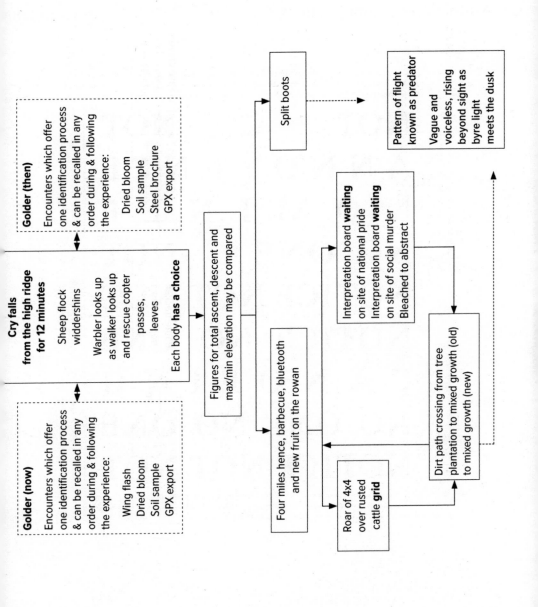

Golder (then)

Encounters which offer one identification process & can be recalled in any order during & following the experience:

Dried bloom
Soil sample
Steel brochure
GPX export

Cry falls
from the high ridge
for 12 minutes

Sheep flock widdershins

Warbler looks up as walker looks up and rescue copter passes, leaves

Each body **has a choice**

Golder (now)

Encounters which offer one identification process & can be recalled in any order during & following the experience:

Wing flash
Dried bloom
Soil sample
GPX export

Split boots

Pattern of flight known as predator

Vague and voiceless, rising beyond sight as byre light meets the dusk

Figures for total ascent, descent and max/min elevation may be compared

Interpretation board **waiting** on site of national pride
Interpretation board **waiting** on site of social murder
Bleached to abstract

Four miles hence, barbecue, bluetooth and new fruit on the rowan

Dirt path crossing from tree plantation to mixed growth (old) to mixed growth (new)

Roar of 4x4 over rusted cattle **grid**

regulating / referred conferred referred referred makes following // means is owned occupied managed is has
is used connected foregoing include / means has undertaken carry out relating / means extending amending /
means comprising is organised has had organised include advertised operating messaging / means committed

/ dipping is taken should be returned / shall / dam obstruct / take catch injure destroy disturb fishing / pollute / shall go
formed intimating is do is displayed // entering leaving designated transporting require / permitted must be driven must
obstruct risk causing must exceed / parking provided are are being used are parking reserves impose parking /

is cause using / means authorised // shall / enter leave / enter remain closed / commit / enter authorised do / damage
remove / leave provided / obstruct / carry discharge / bring deposit leave cause / smoke prohibiting // may refuse shall
dispersed / may make exempting would include has believe used said result / congregates is cause is empowered take ensure

NOT the law rises from the horizon NOT

ANNOYANCE

NOMINEE

NO ONE NOT

NOTICE NOT NOT

NOTICE NO ONE

CANOEING

NO ONE NO ONE

NOTICE NOT NOT

the rain answers its naming

disturb ill-treat injure take destroy / set use taking // canoeing rafting rowing sailing swimming are managed
posted must be kept is respond is is responded deposited / ensure is picked removed deposited / shall / exercise / displace
is dispersed may include taking seeking required / is is suffered occasioned take suffered was // allowed is

parking is allowed / abandoned parked parked designated parking parked foregoing causing removed stored displayed // cycling / cycling designated / must maintain ensure do endanger should exceed // shall / camp / light / are allowed provided is paid must be removed // be sold supplied granted / consumed prohibiting

NOT NOT NOT

NO ONE CANNOT

CANNOT NO ONE

NO NOTICE NO

NOTICE NO

each breath expands my body of work

NO ONE NOTICE

NOTICE NOTICE

NO ONE NOT

NOTICE NOT

rewritten by the day's bright eye

Left vertical margin: / walking / training make use / seeking use care / guided made / is // reserves levy use provided shall alter / is required use use designated growing may levy use // has believing contravened contravening contravene foregoing expel exclude / contravenes attempts contravene foregoing is contavene made exceeding / is expelled excluded fails leave re-enters shall be

Right vertical margin: designated / is shall enter remain // shall agreeing comply issued / organise take part / display distribute advertising / organise participate betting gaming / recruit drill practice / use controlled / play practice / play practice / leave / make landing / shall / use play indicating / solicit collect / use is is detecting is issued detecting detecting / geocaching is

Bottom margin (inverted): beat shake sweep brush cleanse / shall / sell hire / carry / beg solicit / shall include are limited following assisted using / erect / erect affix / erect attach entitled remove shall pay / dispose cremated deceased / hang allowed geocaching is followed / shall operate play play amplified // shall / enter reserved use accompanied

I was having a quiet dinner with my friends when J____ C_____ appeared. We had not invited her, but on the other hand we had laid the table for six when only five of us girls were expected, and there was plenty of roast fowl to go around. 'Sit down, p l e a s e

my good friend Hera collapsed. She was never a strong one. Hyssop, who had been reading a zine on contemporary witchcraft, grabbed the two-volume Library of America boxed edition of Ursula K. Le Guin's Hainish Cycle from my IKEA bookshelf and uttered a hex

and the three suns chased each other violently across the sky. J____ laid her hot hot hands on my broad bare shoulders and I felt each drop of oestrogen depart my body, leaving no sex hormones in circulation at all. My bones would break. In mere years my bones would break, and in every third floor flat across this rapidly gentrifying quarter of our fortress city J____ C_____ was appearing. Oh J____. She released the children from the cage of the future. Our Lady of Grief. A bell! A bell! A bell! A bell! A bell! A bell! And then

his breast and his arms of silver · and thou shalt t

ast · even the sea mo

C_____

sit down,' I said and cut off a slice for J____ C_____'s Portmeirion special edition plate. She did not sit down; she gestured towards the erotic prints hung unevenly on my wall and her jaw opened and closed, as if chewing with her mouth open, but there was n o t h i n g in her mouth to chew. It was then we began to suspect that J____ C_____ was a ghost, which she confirmed by plunging her two hands through the pine-effect tabletop and screaming. Such screams! There was char on the wings. At that p o i n t

of binding; J____ reached over and snapped her neck. Poor Hyssop. Her tits had only just come in and barely any time to enjoy them. A scent of old roses. The wall of my combined living and dining room was all windows and through those unwashed windows the good moons

all was calm and neither Hera nor Hyssop was dead. There were only five seats at the table. No children were taken. Our quiet conversation resumed with small revelations of gentleness. One moon, one sun, and by my left hand my phone screen glowed pure blue.

...reast · with the wave breast and heave shoulder cut off shall not enter into the con... green and the oil ... he that is wounded in the stones or hath his privy member cut off shall not enter into the congregation ... and shalt suck the breast of kings

which also leaned ... toward the pages of ... yes, I spit out an awful ...

```
I   t   o   5   m   g
3   I       2       o
I o t o 2 o m g
6               o
I   t   o   2   m   g
9               3
I   .   2   5       g
o               o
2   t   o   4       g
o               2
I       o   m   c   g
3           4       9
o   .   o   5   m   g
o               2
I . 5 t o 2 m g
2   6   9       o
I   t   o   2   m   g
o               5
I o t o 2 o m g
I       7       8
I   t   o   2   m   g
o               5
I o t o 2 o m g
2       3       o
I   t   o   2   m   g
o               2
3       o   m       g
```

Here is my prayer:
that you will die
after a long & happy life
& when you ascend & pass
through the gates & greet
the recording angel & ask
'Was I right? Was it
right, what I did?',
your face still pinned by shame,
she will say, 'What?
Oh, well . . . we'll check . . .'
& lead you to the Hall of Lives
explaining with gentle hesitance
that records without consequence
are only kept for five years before
dissolution into the stuff of being,
& that after half an hour of searching
& checking her watch she will say,
'I'm sorry, I'm afraid my shift's over,
but feel free to stay.
I'm sure you're here somewhere.'
& that you will look up
at the not-quite-infinite-
but-always-expanding
stacks of meaning,
the tall rolling ladders,
& never learn how to leave.

glides over sea or back and forth along bre
do not pass it on to others. It may harm them
note that individual variation leads t
if your symptoms seriously hinder
single birds often fly low over the w
you are at an increased risk of fract
somewhat more elastic and fast without i
ask you about your own and your family's
communally in winter. Food
the benefits and risks of continuing with
usually alternates between a quic
if you are not sure about any o
highly vocal, often heard at
stop using it at once and co
occasionally so strong as to
a history of excessive grow
plain, very pale grey ab
if you still have your womb
rather plain head with di
you will have a bleed once a month (so-ca
upperparts and underparts i
important that you inform the nurse/h
unmistakeable in flight: broad white
and if one travels to the lungs, it can ca
a shallow depression, defended with fierce
will not prevent memory loss. There is
keeps watch from top of island or

Benison

ixed solution in sealed vials in an autoclave
l years ago in this remote archipelago
ting new rules, no matter how unreasonable
four monuments that make up the Heart
ise to use controlled airflow and filtering
evidence of the material and spiritual
ccuser doesn't want to think that chemical
iving standing stones of the elliptical
terrile, I sterilize everything as the final stage
se passage points close to midwinter
k of dust lands in one of hundred
within a vast topographic bowl
bbles float in the solution for days
ttings. The wealth of contemporary burial

Little me winning
a sharpener for knowing
the answer is hell
to the question where
will you go for being
in such low fashion, you
were wrong: hell is
where you are, knowing
such an answer.
Be not afraid, bright one!
Years turn against the blade,
sulphur turns all to gold, & hell
is where you grow possible.
You're already here.

11, 8, 13, 12, 16, 16
11, 11, 9, 11, 27, 8, 15
12, 11, 11, 12, 11, 7, 8
13, 11, 13, 20, 16, 18
9, 8, 12, 8, 8, 14, 17
20, 32, 16, 17, 17, 17
38, 17, 24, 35, 36, 18
24, 17(EMS), 19, 36
26, 25, 25, 26, 26, 27
31, 12, 17, 28, 13, 28
28, 12, 29, 15, 11, 34
26, 13, 15, 13, 23, 27
16, 27, 28, 16, 16, 16
16, 18, 18, 15, 15, 16

The Reasonable People

The reasonable people are coming. The reasonable people have eyes and mouths. The reasonable people remember their lessons. The reasonable people have a few questions for them. The reasonable people are on the waiting list for stray dog adoption. The reasonable people have proved their suitability. The reasonable people are worried. The reasonable people have concerns. The concerns are reasonable. The reasonable people began asking questions. The reasonable people went to one meeting. The protest outside was not reasonable. The protest frightened the reasonable people. The reasonable people were never political before. The reasonable people think it's important to weigh the arguments. The reasonable people say it's such a shame that things have become so heated. The reasonable people have chapped hands from so much washing. The reasonable people are inspired. It has been a long time since the reasonable people went dancing. The reasonable people are hopeful. The reasonable people are learning so much. The reasonable people believe in public service. The reasonable

people are
on public
boards. The
reasonable
people are
people
hold an
investigation.
The
reasonable
role. The
reasonable
people just
want to give
everyone
away from
it all. The
reasonable
people miss
coffee
internet
forums at
11pm looking
for advice on
their

proud of their
positions
on public
boards. The
reasonable
people are
cleared by the
investigation.
The
investigation
involved a
hug. The
reasonable
people list
everything
-mornings.
The
reasonable
people have
lost their
unsleeping
children. The
reasonable
people are on
internet

people
suggest they
do not enter
the building.
The
was
reasonable.
The
reasonable
people call
they have
done for
them. The
reasonable
people have
pencil
sharpeners
The
reasonable
people have
forums at
11.30pm
discussing the
cracks in their
bodies.

reasonable
people are
treasurers.
The
reasonable
HR. The
reasonable
people do not
believe it is
the funder's
blocked
them. The
reasonable
people just
want to get
beautiful
singing
voices. The
reasonable
people are on
The
reasonable
people are
on internet
forums at

midnight

planning a
       abuse. The
    bullying. The reasonable   against
letter-writing
campaign The reasonable but people think mums. The
about reasonable people think they have a reasonable
   that no... prejudice people ask... able
  people read   notes people are
  should this time reasonable people are
the reasonable
  people say round. The people email afraid of
   that they reasonable at them. The. The
     them at 3am
   believe in people say to say they are reasonable
reasonable   that they have people have
  violence. The   not safe.
  people ask orchestrated building a been abused.
  what is a campaign temple on The
  wrong with reasonable reasonable the hill. The
  them. The people people have reasonable
   have been columns. The people go for
reasonable threatened. reasonable
people have The reasonable
been abused   people are
    people would
on social pressed never. The never
media. The long flowers. The reasonable advocate for
walks. The reasonable people would policies of
reasonable people would elimination,
people have never. The but they
collections of

policies The reasonable
understand exist. The reasonable early
The people
and reasonable people this year. The
reasonable people parade too
sympathize sympathize reasonable
people understand people say
with understand people
heroes people those
reasons institution may the
reasonable people may offer
is rights Christmas
crowd campaign support. The
reasonable
a lucid medicine people
identify poor. reasonable people
The reasonable promise to
reasonable publish The be hard to
editorials. reasonable.
people do not people get their
The people give
speak their publish names right.
out awards.
name. The editorials
The
about abuse.

[47]

reasonable
people are
afraid of
being
silenced. The

reasonable
people do
not condone
prejudice and
hatred. The

The
reasonable
people will
not meet with
them to

reasonable
people
think their
overreaction
is dangerous.

people are
afraid of
dentists. The
reasonable
people try

talk. The
reasonable
people will
not apologise.
The

reasonable
people are
defending
liberty. The
reasonable

people think
it's just
Question
Time. The
common
reasonable
sense. The
reasonable

very hard
to go to
the dentist
regularly but
then, you
The
reasonable
people have
persistent

know, this
sinus
pandemic.
infections are
The
embarrassed
when they
reasonable
phone their
people watch
GPs,

people demonstrate
as is the
precious
GPs.

the takeover
of the

internal
their GPs
machinery of
recommend
the party of
menthol
sweets. The
reasonable
reasonable
people enjoy
crime fiction.
The

people make
a bulk order
of menthol
sweets on
Amazon. The

reasonable
people have
many, many
limbs. The
reasonable
people are
just worried
about the
integrity of
their body.

resource of
NHS time,

[48]

died last
week. The
reasonable
people believe
that

reasonable
people take
powereasonable
powerpeople's
reasonfavourite
succulents

polarisation
is dangerous.
The
reasonable
people are

walking down
the street.
The
reasonable   alive with
people are   light. The
                reasonable
                people are at
                the door. The

reasonable
people are
singing. The
reasonable
people are

coming.
The
reasonable
people are
here.

[49]

[breathe in]

Out of Existence

Suite for Solo Voice or Chorus

1. **AGP.** Allegro moderato.
2. **GID.** Adagio (costante).
3. **TIM.** Presto.
4. **EGG.** Largo.
5. **GRA.** Andante.

This music may only be sung
by those to whom these terms are given.

AGP

Allegro moderato.

au   au   au   au

au   au   au   au

au   au   au   au

au   au   au   au

au   no   au   no   au   no   au   no

au   no   au   no   au   no   au   no

au hi no gy   au hi no gy   au hi no gy   au hi no gy

phile   phile   phile   phile

au   au   au   au

no   no   no   no phi gy

au   au   au   au

no   hi gy no   no   hi gy no

au to   au to   au to   au to to to

t honestly . . . no shit . . . its really a goal of mine and someting i activly werk at to eventually b
mpassion y'know wut i mean?? the ultimate beauty being beauty that has had to proove its met

no to hi gy   no to hi gy   no to hi gy   no to to to

au to   au to   au to   au to to to

phile   phile   phile   phile

[52]

au   au   au   au

au au   au to   no to   no no

gy   no   au no   gy   to   au to no

hi   no hi to   no gy no   no

au   no to au   no   au hi no

no gy   no hi no   no

au hi no gy hi hi no gy phi hi no gy

phi phile   phi phile   phi phi phile

no   no

no   no no   no no   no no

no to   no to   no to

no to   no no to   no no to   no no to to to

no to hi gy no to hi gy no to hy gi no to to no

no to   no no to   no no to   no no to to to

no to hi gy no to hi gy no to to no

phile   phile   phile   phile

We learn about worlds when being accommodated can be put through the struggles we have to question worlds, when we are becomes a place you reside in, question: explanations you must to make sense or navigate your as familiar landscapes no long question is to be thrown into a as startling. Another way of so home, when we are asked when even what we are, we experien hammering away at our being. is to be given a hammer, a tool away at the surfaces of what is

give myself full sexually to some manifestation of absolute horror/ darkness (but with a tinge o, the most deepest beauty being the beauty that was lifted from the ugliest of places ??? thats the ki

[53]

Constante.

ssssssssssssssssssssO! ffffffffffffffffa! ssssssssssssssssssssssssssO! ffffffffffffffffa! sssssssssssssssssssssssssssO! ffffffffffffffffa! ssssssssssssssssssssssssssssO! ffffffffffffffffa! sssssssssssssssssssssssssssssO! ffffffffffffffffa! ssssssssssssssssssssssssssssssO! ffffffffffffffffa! sssssssssssssssssssssssssssssssO! ffffffffffffffffa! sssssssssO!

Because the card carries such furious s

*The right
payload
delivered at
the proper
angle.*

Adagio.

?:dys-pho-ri-a-a-a-a-a-a-a-aaaaa-a-a-adaaa-a-aa-a-a-a-a-a-a-aa-8-oo-8-8oo8-8oo8-8oooo-8-dis-8-o8o8-8oooo-o-

e many people recoil at the sight of it.

aa-aa-aaa-a-a-a-a-a-aa-aa-a-
-aa-aa-aaa-a-aa-a-aa-a-aa-aa
-aa-aa-aaaaaaa-8-8-8o-8r-der:o-c
a-o-o-8-o8oo8-8-8o-8o-o
o-o-o8oo-o8oo8

During
revolution, we
hold onto our
definitions of
home while we
destroy the
foundation
that no longer
supports us.

[55]

TIM

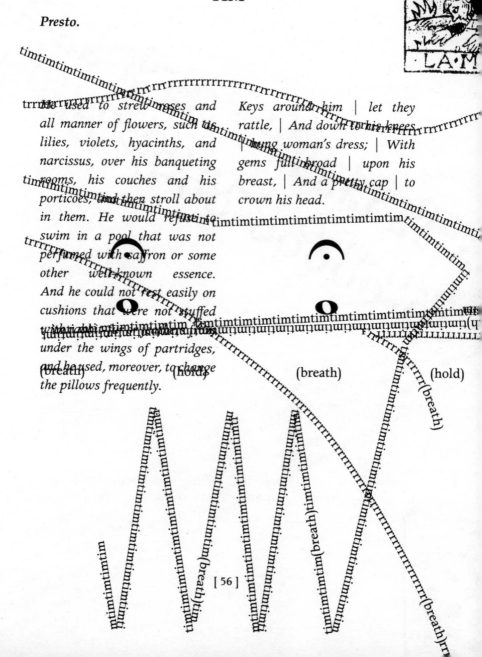

Presto.

He used to strew roses and all manner of flowers, such as lilies, violets, hyacinths, and narcissus, over his banqueting rooms, his couches and his porticoes, and then stroll about in them. He would refuse to swim in a pool that was not perfumed with saffron or some other well-known essence. And he could not rest easily on cushions that were not stuffed with rabbit fur or feathers from under the wings of partridges, and used, moreover, to change the pillows frequently.

Keys around him | let they rattle, | And down to his knees | hung woman's dress; | With gems full broad | upon his breast, | And a pretty cap | to crown his head.

(breath)   (holds)   (breath)   (hold)

(breath)   (breath)   (breath)

[56]

(breath)

The long-haired priest of Rhea,   And then he had the nun |
the newly gelded, the dancer   brought out and stripped | and
from Lydian Tmolus whose   he ordered Silence stripped. |
shriek is heard afar | dedicates,   Just as Merlin had said: | all
now he rests from his frenzy, to   was found there for all.
the solemn Mother who dwells
by the banks of Sangarius these
tambourines, | his scourge
armed with bones, these noisy
brazen cymbals, and a scented
lock of his hair.

(breath)   timtimtimtimtimtimtim   (hold)   (breath)   (hold)
timtimtimtimtimtimtimtimtimtimtim(breath)tim timtimtimtimtimti

The number of repetitions of 'tim' and the length of the trill is
not precise: rather, the singer continues until fully out of breath,
physically unable to keep going. Strain is heard. There is the
minimum possible interval between the breath and resuming song.

In chorus, each singer proceeds at their own pace and ceases after
the fourth breath. Each waits for every singer to cease before all
begin the next verse together.

EGG

Largo.

sh		br		ck		f
mh		ck		gg		m
sh		tr		p		qu
br		n		qu		ck
sh	i	br		p	ə	qu
m		ck	i	gg	e	i	f
sh	i	tr		ck		ə	m
br	e	e	n	i	i	qu	i	ck

shick brim ef   fam fick   queep ef   figg   queesh em
shin fin   brim fin   fick trash   trash shish
queef brish ef   brigg   em en fip   fap
tram brish tram track brim fim tragg em fig queef treen
shish track brish tram brim brish en tragg trash treen pap nap
shick brish brish shick brish brap track tragg trash tragg pap ship
treen ship shep   trick   treg tregg trish treen queen
shap   mick fick pick shap ship shep

sh		br		ck		f
mh		ck		gg		m
sh		tr		p		qu
br		n		qu		ck
sh	i	br		p	ə	qu
m		ck	i	gg	e	i	f
sh	i	tr		ck		ə	m
br	e	e	n	i	i	qu	i	ck

delicatamente decise delicatamente

rrr

shick brim ef   fam fick queep   ef   figg   queesh em
shin fin   brim fin fick   trash   trash   shish
queef brish ef   brigg   em en fip   fap
tram brish tram track brim fim   tragg em tragg fig queef
shish tram brish brish tram brim brish brap en tragg tragg trash treen treen
shick brish a brish   shick brish e brish track tragg trash   tragg pap nap
treen   trick   treg i tregg trish   treen pap e ship a
shap a ship a shep a   mick fick i pick   shap a ship a shep a   queen

sh   ck
mh   gg
sh   p
br   qu
sh   p
m   gg   i
sh   ck
br   qu   e e e e e

shick brim ef fick   fam fick queep   ef quip figg   queesh kreem em track
shin fin fick   brim fin fick   trash track track trash track shish track
queef if if   brigg if if queep   em en fip   fap shish treen
tram brish tram em track brim fim queep   tragg em tragg fig queef trim trim treen
shish tram brish brish   tram brim brish brap en tragg tragg trash treen trim
shick brim brish quip   shick brish nick feg track tragg tregg trish tragg pap nap
treen ship shep   trick nick pick   treg ship ship   treen pap ship
shap   mick fick pick   shap ship shep   queen

vittorioso delicatamente **bellicoso**

o with this shit

GRA

Andante.

Invert! Invert! Invert! Invert! Invert!

INVERT! INVERT! INVERT! INVERT! INVERT!

Invert! Invert! Invert! Invert! Invert!

INVERT! INVERT! INVERT! INVERT! INVERT!

Invert! Invert! Invert! Invert! Invert!

INVERT! INVERT! INVERT! INVERT! INVERT!

Invert! Invert! Invert! Invert! Invert!

INVERT! INVERT! INVERT! INVERT! INVERT!

Invert! Invert! Invert! Invert! Invert!

INVERT! INVERT! INVERT! INVERT! INVERT!

Invert! Invert! Invert! Invert! Invert!

INVERT! INVERT! INVERT! INVERT! INVERT!

Invert! Invert! Invert! Invert! Invert!

INVERT! INVERT! INVERT! INVERT! INVERT!

They are good, these doctors —
of them very good; they work
trying to solve our problem, b
the time they must work in th
— the whole truth is known on
normal invert. The doctors
make the ignorant think
hope to bring home the su
millions; only one of ou
some do that . . .

Giant women stride the skyline,
lumbering gangly war machines,
tattooed[1] and regimentalized, skin
dyed[2], double jointed grappling
limbs, covered in eyebrows, their head
has none, they lope like spider dogs,
pointed rudimentary breasts, barbs
between their legs[3], they spurt caustic
fluid when damaged.

are always lying in wait

ERT!
!Invert!
INVERT! INVERT!
Invert! Invert!
INVERT! INVERT!

Invert!

[breathe out]

The Hills

thrusts holds
peaks passes
closes undiscloses
the many-gendered mountain

feet on the ridge
fingers on the spine
sweat in the crevices
sweet in the lungs

cloud a firm
kind warning
not today friend
maybe ever

refreshing the weather
needing different news
refreshing the summit
finding different news

the cry of an eagle
or the cry of someone
crying like an eagle
or the cry of someone
hoping for an eagle

cloud a stone's
opening lungs
will you keep
going

a tumbling pebble
for an open mouth
a hot stream
for a giving corrie

the bottom
imagining greeting
the top
greeting

cloud a bone
white challenge
what's in me
dare you

[66]

a stick in the hand
sticking to the hand
marking the skin
making a path

water in the air
water in the eyes
water in the boots
water on the thighs

cloud a word
light-translated
say that again
louder

the mouth spreads
its breath
the mounth spreads
its breadth

the line of the trail
breaks the scree
the line of the burn
breaks the skin

cloud a voice
less shape
of
wanting

wind across the face
belt across the flank
rain across the brow
beating the crown

mounting the summit
to make more summits
crossing the saddle
to slake a thirst

cloud a herd
of pale horses
calling
out

crags in the fog
ships in the reek
steps in the spate
waves in the rock

the cry of an ending
or the cry of someone
crying like an ending
or the cry of someone
hoping for an ending

cloud a throne
for a raven
silent
as a knife

the path behind
here and there
the path ahead
now and then

one foot in front of the other
until there's a meaning
one word in front of the other
until there's a meeting

cloud a point
to speir and be speired
moving with
the moving mountain

CAN NOT FIND WHAT YOU ARE

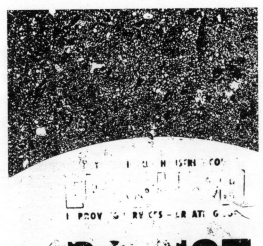

Against Waiting

after Thomas Clark

BELFAST KOI: UNKNOWN # GENDERKIT.ORG.UK # ? + MONTHS 59 :BELFAST

#CARDIFF: 20 MONTHS + ? # TRANSHEALTHUK.NOBLOGS.ORG # EDINBURGH: 38 MONTHS + ? #

Late at night, every night, I am stuck, with the most impossible baggage, and recover the world.

It is impossible to accept all the coercion, violence, property, triviality, to stay home.

That nothing ends with my body and my work, so closed, so grudgingly unavailable, is my little curse.

Waiting is a monstrous way of giving in.

From time to time and place to place there are people waiting, their sky blocked with stairs, seen and unseen, strange and broken.

I wait when I fall in my own tracks, wait when I begin to uncensor parts of myself.

Destinations obscure their journeys, those few inches spat out, but waiting disorganises itself, partial to any line beyond the map.

I'll see nothing if I go there.

Waiting is a stationary form of walking.

What we give, what we stay with, is more important than what we take from the map.

Waiting, broken, is a bad way to be found.

The closest places are inaccessible once one is stuck.

Vindications, demands and facts are waters rising over good ramps.

When I am waiting, I lose everything about myself and about those stuck with me.

When we spend the night exhausted we cannot talk, when we spend it horribly awake we cannot walk.

The length of the wait reveals the infinity and oneness of hidden things, from the thin body at depression's limits to the forest's homeless giant, and the depth of neglect we will be given to bear.

A soft hollow, an opening, an expanding lung, nothing that turns me into my presence is a bad thing in a wait.

Directions, charging forward, noise and definition, all come from this place of detached indifference.

What exactly I refuse is close to meaningless.

The poorest places are the most crowded.

Waiting is unjust and enforced; I am a waiting fool and both sides of the fence are as bad as each other.

Waiting is as much unreasoning as true.

The mouth of a wait cannot speak, an unkind silence.

Stops, doors and crowded breaths have unnatural speed.

We know the shape of a wait when it is shared and familiar, when it is homely; so it must also be strange, singular, what can't be done.

Endless waiting, out of weather, out of season, is a door or break through which the most uncertain losses silently escape.

A wheel of nylon or rubber, newly stolen, will roll over the road.

Of the few ways out of a trap, I am not offered, ever, all of them, and the challenge of waiting is to become merciless, intolerant of the reasons for the offer I receive, to refuse the offered exit rather than to affirm equality.

Many end a short wait not with giving up but with enmity.

Clear skies, sun, warmth, when I have fallen in these I have lost much of the dream of air and breath.

A night, from dusk to dawn, is the unnatural extreme of waiting.

An interesting wait is stolen.

To wait for a moment in a busy day is to lose a little ignorance.

Against false humanity, experience must travel from the body to some other reality.

Closing, cloaking, shaking, choking, are all the same as waiting.

Falling down, the surroundings close in; rising, the floor races away.

I cannot offer a wait which isn't an index of such burdens: the exhausted weight of the underground; the dense weight of the paved road; the hungry weight beneath even skies.

I cannot wait in one place and not break all links to myself, take myself into cool isolation, pushing strangers far away.

There are waits in which we find ourselves, waits in which we leave ourselves again.

Is there nothing worse than to be in, waiting, beyond the strange earth?

Ghost Highland Way

To print, write or step.

When there are choices, choose at random. Each phrase needs its space. A star makes a break on either side.

Print 'The wey raxes oot afore ye. Ye dinna hae lang.' and a star.

Set the limit to a number between six and ten. Begin the count at one.

The cycle begins here.

Print {DAY} and {NIGHT}.

> To print DAY: print {TIME}, {MOOD}, {PLACE}, a break, {WEATHER}, {LAND}, {LIFE}, a break, {FADE}, a break, 'Sundoun.' and a star.

>> To print TIME: if the count has reached your limit, print {END}, else, if the count is one, print 'The first day', if two, 'The seicont day', if three, 'The thrid day', if four, 'The fowert day', if five, 'The fift day', if six, 'The saxt day', if seven, 'The seivent day', if eight, 'The echt day', if nine, 'The nint day', if ten, 'The tent day'.

>> To print MOOD: print one of 'gangs slaw', 'gangs caum', 'gangs lither', 'gangs brisk', 'weirs awa', 'is cauld', 'is cauld-kin', 'is oorie', 'is snell', 'is growthie', 'is dreich', 'is wairm', 'is muithie', 'is het', 'is sweltrie', 'is frozen', 'flowes like hinnie', 'is a sair pech', 'hurts', 'lilts', 'rants', 'dances', 'babbers', 'birls', 'shaks', 'sowfs', 'daffs like a foggie-bummer', 'seems unpossible', 'seems unlikely', 'seems

fremmit', 'seems fey', 'is like ony ither', 'is like ony ither', 'is like ony ither', 'is like ony ither', 'smells o heather', 'smells o yird', 'smells o gress', 'smells o peat' or 'smells o smeuk', then a stop.

To print PLACE: print 'Ye', {MOVEMENT}, {RELATION}, {LIKENESS}, {MARK} and a stop.

To print MOVEMENT: print one of 'drift', 'fleet', 'paunder', 'daver', 'gove', 'haik', 'sloom', 'swither' or 'waff'.

To print RELATION: print one of 'by', 'naur', 'past', 'ower' or 'throu'.

To print LIKENESS: print one of 'a braken', 'a ruint', 'a brunt', 'an empie', 'a cleart', 'a cleart', 'a cleart', 'a deid', 'a lost', 'a voidit', 'a sleepin', 'an auld', 'the banes o a', 'the wrack o a', 'the signs o a', 'the merk o a' or 'the scaur o a'.

To print MARK: print one of 'kirk', 'skeul', 'toun', 'bothy', 'shielin', 'steidin', 'croft', 'biggin', 'fauld', 'fort', 'broch', 'dam', 'station', 'manor', 'camp grund', 'lodge', 'hotel', 'caur', 'train', 'lorry', 'cairt', 'motorwey', 'viaduct' or 'bridge'.

To print WEATHER: print one of 'A smuir o rain', 'A daud o rain', 'A wattergaw', 'A rainbowe', 'The cairies scud', 'The cloods draw in', 'Reid sun', 'Atter cloods', 'Burnin rain', 'An onding', 'A scoor', 'The sun bides a stoond', 'Mackerel sky', 'Haird winds', 'A reezin wind', 'Ess, fawin', 'Ice on the air', 'A saut souch', 'The rain nivver gies ower', 'Thick rouk', 'Cranreuch', 'Hullerie', 'Paulie ure', 'Here an thare,

[85]

sun', 'Bytimes, rain', 'Snell gowsts tug at ye', 'Wind teirs ye', 'Awmaist snaw', 'A deek o sun', 'Smeuk on the wind', 'Rain an sun', 'Wind an rain', 'Sun an wind', nothing, nothing or nothing, then a stop.

To print LAND: print one of 'A scaur on the brae', 'A cairn', 'A bank o rannoch', 'A path lined wi rosebay willaeherb', 'Airchin rowan', 'A field o stumps', 'A shingle bi the watter', 'Great boolders', 'A scaur on the knowe', 'A cairn', 'The heimaist peak', 'The reek o ile', 'Snaw on the ben-heid', 'Granite', 'Trees turnin', 'Skimmerin watter', 'A whimpelt roddin', 'Deid watter', 'Roch staps', 'Glaur', 'Muirland', 'Muirburn', 'Black braes', 'A brent rise', 'A wee burn', 'A bed o heather', 'A hie balloch', nothing, nothing or nothing, then a stop.

To print LIFE: print one of 'A drift o kye shauchles roond ye', 'A willie-whip-the-wind, dancin', 'Ye fleg a flock o sheep', 'A gait hyne awa watches ye', 'Twa craws jink owerheid', 'An eagle draps', 'A fir faws on the ither side o the brae', 'A train thunners awa, oot o sicht', 'Gunshot', 'The roar o stags', 'The roar o injines', 'Lauchter on the wind', 'Ye daidle by a linn', 'Ye watch the fells', 'Ye bield in a howe', 'Ye tak hicht', 'Ye haud at', 'Ye pass', 'Ye watch a gollach mak her wey', 'Ye bore at the stanes', 'Ye speir at the sky', 'Ye reck the yird', nothing, nothing, nothing, nothing or nothing, then a stop.

To print FADE: if the count is two lower than the limit, print 'Yer time draws close. Thare a lang wey yet.', else if the count is one lower than the limit, print 'Yer time is nearly ower. Ye arena thare.', else print nothing.

[86]

To print NIGHT: print {BED}, {DREAM}, a break, 'Skybrek.' and a star, then increase the count by one and return to the beginning of the cycle.

To print BED: print one of 'A bed o heather', 'The cauld grund', 'The saft yird', 'Aneath an aik', 'Amang the pines', 'Anunder the starns', 'A braken ruif', 'A howe', 'I'the haily-muild', 'A sithean', then a stop.

To print DREAM: print 'Ye dream o', {DESIRE}, {DESTINATION} and a break.

To print DESIRE: print one of 'yer wants', 'yer needs', 'yer greenins', 'whit ye ettle efter', 'yer howps', 'yer lists', 'roads ithoot end', 'clims ithoot summits', 'seas ithoot shores', 'boats ithoot airs', 'tours ithoot stairs', 'castles ithoot doors', 'mendin', 'pleisance', 'hale-heiditness', or 'rest', then a stop.

To print DESTINATION: print one of 'A wairm fire', 'A guid howff', 'A full plate', 'Appen gates', 'Appen airms', 'The bricht toun', 'The gowd licht', 'The hie keep', 'The lang sleep', 'Yer fowk', 'Yer fowk', 'Eneuch', 'Eneuch', nothing, nothing or nothing, then a stop.

To print END: print 'Yer time is ower. Ye coudna find it. Ye dwyne awa. Anither year, mebbe?' and immediately leave the cycle.

The cycle ends here.

Again?

No Such Thing as Belonging

If home is an island, build a bridge
    of spit and hairclips. If home
is a mobile phone, drop it on a concrete
    trampoline. If a party,
snap the lights on. If a bed, strip.

    If home is a yoga mat, plant it
in the gutter. If a bank balance,
    hook it up to a vampire's drip.
If a hilltop, prank call the mountain
    removal service. If a book,

burn another book. If home is a game,
    rage quit short of the boss.
If a download, delete. But if home is a pigeon,
    feed it seed, for pigeons have it hard enough
and have a deal to teach.

If home is a kitchen, torch dinner.
If a pair of boots, detach your feet.
    If a car, give a meadow.
If a river, give a dam. If home is a knife,
    sharpen it first (it's safer),

and if home is a knife, keep breathing and do
    what you do until home is not a knife.
If a pill, chew. If a drink, spew.
    If a plate, bite through to the bone.
If a mistake, undo, undo, undo.

    If home is a small grey room,
brew in your gut a grander room.
    If empty, fill. If full, spill.
If there is no home, take it with you.
    And if home is an island, build a bridge.

Don't Let the Poets See This

the breathing forest / the shyness of the crown
earth is getting a black box / under a tree's root system
pollinated by beetles / together in the spring
a language similar to humans / on their migration to the moon

an ice-encaged rose / fireflies plus long exposure
the recent lava flow in iceland / the star-shaped sand of okinawa
the glistening waters of jamaica / butterflies drinking turtle tears
lake michigan after an ice storm / soft serve outside greenwich
    observatory
they fall hard / back into existence

a piece of your childhood / looking at myself in the mirror
something came in the night / i finally saw the moon
my clearest picture of a third quarter moon / the problem with
    the moon
the sexual tension between the moon and the ocean / the
    supermoon freed the container ship
down her throat by lunchtime / some satellites just can't be caged

clipboards at the laundromat / seventy four gigabytes of data
a photocopy of her phone / writing poems isn't activism
media not displayed / never going to emotionally recover
this image has been removed in response to a report from the
    copyright holder

Signs

when deep in the landfill the servers awake to weird noises
and diligent winds drop their trade to ask where they're going
and ruminant mountains are steadily making new choices

the screens crack up citywide with the stories they're showing
and circles of well-dressed stones make troubling findings
and couplets and triplets grow strange in the heat of their knowing

but nothing's as queer or as true as a theory unwinding
held in the kinship of ragged and rude-soft voices
the easy and free-tongued choir of the earth and its minding

A Stone

A heart that beats very slowly.

A Heart

A stone that breaks twice a second.

Elegy

i.m. Brianna Ghey 2006–2023

Sister, you are smiling when I meet you,
half a bar of chocolate held between
your thumb and half-raised middle finger, so
at first I think you're offering the camera
a grain of fuck off magic with your grin.
But no, the eager sun is only melting
a lick of sugar down your wrist. The grass
is only watered. Your brows are only plucked.

Sister, I meant to meet you in the pit
of punks, girls to the front. I meant to brace
my marching voice on yours, our shivered longing
hoarse as rafters. I meant a moonstruck dress
my bones outgrew to settle on your shoulders.
I meant to sleep. I meant only to stay
safe in distant sisterhood. Now
it's already morning and the dogs of news

are rattling the gate before your blood
has sunk into the earth. The fife and drum.
The column's inch. The typing has begun.
My sister, when I call to pass the dead
weight from my heart to hers, says, 'The worst
is hoping to hear that it wasn't . . .' But when my sisters
walk with ghosts on either side, what odds
does it make: chance or choice, the edge of hatred

finds its mark. Sister, you were born
after I first ringed my eyes with black,
after I first skinned the street and tasted
desperation, after womanhood
began to ring her furious alarms
beyond my reach. I wrote a bloody book
before you took a breath. The space you left
cannot be filled, though we, your hungered sisters,

will drown the world-tree with grief. How dare a death
be made to mean more than its cut to meaning?
How dare a poem be? Am I no different
from the coursers ripping at your years?
I turn to words to turn your loss to less
than unspeakable. I too have my devices.
Sister, you are far from the first sister
I've had to make a way to grieve — familiar

sorrows sing familiar staves — but you
deserve far better than the anaesthesia
binding my limbs, than vigils, than editing.
Sister, I am sorry. Sister, the spells
you taught yourself to shape yourself anew
could level kingdoms, but all I wish for you
is life. Here, this is my small flame.
Sister, I will always carry your name.

Volume

This stane is loud. In his hollow rubbit
intae a bigger stane, hid hides loud.
The hollow is loud, the bigger staen, loud;
the tide twal fit awa turnan here
on his twice-daily haund is loud. Loud,
the rich spreid o tangle: loud, the trickle
o sturry frae the field abuin, loud, the runic
track o an oystercatcher in the loud sand; loud,
the three-quarter sun. When there's nae body
tae hear, aa this an more is loud enough
tae make bleed, tae brak bane, tae shake
apairt the unhearin objeck, at's no here.

Credits and Notes

First publications

Some Definitions: Easter Road Press
Them!: Cambridge Literary Review
Materials: Shoreline of Infinity
All the Verbs: Aiblins
The Worker: New Writing Scotland
Redd Ap: Smoke and Mold
Living: nationalcentreforwriting.org.uk
May a Transsexual Hear a Bird?: Cambridge Literary Review
Innumerable Transitional Forms: nls.uk
Found City Poems: foundcitypoems.tumblr.com
A Scan of the Ashes: Sporazine
J____ C____: Hoax
Malison: Re:creation
The Reasonable People: harryjosiegiles.bandcamp.com
Out of Existence: ambf.co.uk/over-at, made with Vivien Holmes
The Hills: Push the Boat Out
Ghost Highland Way: bit.ly/ghosthighlandway
Against Walking: home printer, made with Polly Atkin and Vahni
   Anthony Ezekiel Capildeo
Crush: Push the Boat Out
No Such Thing as Belonging: Young Scot
Signs: When I Was Me
Volume: Irish Pages
Gorgon Love Medley: Scottish Book Trust

Poems may have changed significantly from their original appearance.

Quotations and references, where not given in the text

11: hades.fandom.com; Contrapoints, *Cringe*

15: en.wikipedia.org/wiki/Breathing

26: Tiqqun (tr. Semiotext(e)), *Preliminary Materials for a Theory of the Young-Girl*

27: William Shakespeare, *Sonnet 130*; Carol Ann Duffy, *Mrs Tiresias*

28: Charles Darwin, *On the Origin of Species*

41: Alfred G. Francis, *On a Romano-British Castration Clamp*

42: NHS Scotland, *Gender Reassignment Protocol*

46: kingjamesbibleonline.org

48: A packet of estrogen; *Collins Bird Guide*

49: Lena's lab results; UNESCO, *Heart of Neolithic Orkney*

56: Sara Ahmed, *An Affinity of Hammers*; Sybil Lamb, *How to Get Fucked by a Trans Woman*

58: Rachel Pollack, *Seventy-Eight Degrees of Wisdom*; Cristy C. Road, *Next World Tarot*; Egypt Urnash, *The Tarot of the Silicon Dawn*; Jean Dodal, *Tarot of Marseilles*

60: *Historia Augusta* (tr. D. Magie); *Þrymskviða* (tr. H.A. Bellows); *Greek Anthology* (tr. W.R. Paton); Heldris de Cornuälle, L*e Roman de Silence* (gloss mine)

62: C. Riley Snorton and Jin Haritaworn, *Trans Necropolitics*; Sylvia Rivera, *Y'all Better Quiet Down*

64: John Radclyffe Hall, *The Well of Loneliness*; Porpentine Charity Heartscape, *Psycho Nymph Exile*

82: GIC wait times as collated by Genderkit, April 2023

92: Twitter results for 'don't let poets see this', April 2023

The form of 'Them!' is drawn from Monica Youn's *Study of Two Figures (Pasiphaë/Sado)*, and that of 'Ghost Highland Way' from J.R. Carpenter's *An Ocean of Static*.

Soundtrack (Gorgon Love Medley)

seranine	*I Am Medusa*
100 Gecs	*I Need Help Immediately*
Girls Rituals	*I'm Coiled Like a Snake*
Backxwash	*I Lie Here Buried with My Rings and Dresses*
Lonely Carp	*All My Flowers Rotting in Their Graves*
Planningtorock	*I Wanna Bite Ya*
Deadbit Babe	*I Wanna Be Your Thing*
GODDEXX	*I Want to Shatter in Your Arms*
Macy Rodman	*Love Me!*
Against Me!	*Unconditional Love*
SOPHIE	*L.O.V.E.*
Too Attached	*Love Is Not Love*
AhMerAhSu	*Little Bird*
Comfort	*You're Shaking*
Tami T	*Stay Where You Are*
Ada Rook	*I Don't Want to Hurt You*
In Love With A Ghost	*I Think We Should Break Up*
Left At London	*I Don't Trust U Anymore*
Anohni	*I Don't Love You Anymore*
Uboa	*I Can't Love Anymore*
Ezra Furman	*My Teeth Hurt*
Nervus	*I Wish I Was Dead*
Hormone Cyborg	*I Wish There Was a World for Us*
Wangled Teb	*I Miss You*
Jackie Shane	*I've Really Got the Blues*
Feminazgul	*I Pity the Immortal*
G.L.O.S.S.	*We Live*

Further thanks

AR, Bibi June, Callie, Caspian, Eris, Etzali, Jonathan, Kez,
   Morgan and Sy, for writing a letter with me, and for the care
   that followed.
Alice, Dave, Freddie and Tini, for games night, and for reading
   this book first.
Gabrielle, Jonah, Lyra, and Rachel, for the nourishment.
Innes and Ellie, for going up mountains with me.
Nat, for the long bubble.
Carly, Kara, Rachel, Olivia and Zoe, for sun.
Ash, Juniper, Kit and Sasha, for swimming.
Hava and Maz, for a talking to when it was needed.
Lena and Lilian, for stepping in where the systems fail.
Darcy, again, for everything.